PROCRASTINATION

How to Stop Wasting Your Time and Be More Productive

by George M. Posi

Table of contents

INTRODUCTION

I want to thank you and congratulate you on reading the book "Procrastination: How to stop wasting your time and be more productive." This book contains proven steps and strategies and is a simple guide on how to cure laziness, set goals, improve discipline, control your habits, and end procrastinating.

Procrastination is true quite a menace primarily because it makes you squander time and disregard its importance. That said, the dilemma is that procrastination is something that comes easily to many of us and is a problem that does interfere with our routine chores, performance, and productivity.

Studies show that about 25% to 75% of college students are prone to procrastination when it comes to doing their academic work, and procrastination is a significant reason why often Ph.D. students fail to complete their university dissertations on time. While these statistics pertain to only academics, the truth is procrastination does get in the way of our routine household chores, personal obligations, and even relationships.

Many times, we find ourselves preferring to snuggle in bed over meeting a friend or binge-watching movies instead of doing errands. One way or another, procrastination does influence your life and that too, negatively. So how is it that you can get better control of it and learn to overcome this unhealthy habit? Well, that is what this guide focuses on.

This book gives you a better understanding of the problem at hand, 'procrastination,' and provides you with actionable and practical guidelines on how to control your bad habits, inculcate self-discipline, manage your temptations, set meaningful goals and achieve them with utmost focus and determination.

Thanks again for downloading this book, I hope you enjoy it!

HOW PROCRASTINATION SABOTAGES YOUR LIFE

Even the most organized people do sometimes fritter away hours focused on trivial things like browsing on the internet aimlessly or binge-watching their favorite sitcom on Netflix when they know they should have devoted that very time to something more meaningful.

While on the surface, occasional procrastination is not that harmful, if you become a chronic procrastinator, then it negatively affects your productivity and, eventually, your prosperity and happiness.

Understanding the Basics of Procrastination

Procrastination simply refers to putting away a task for a later time. Therefore, if you are supposed to send an email to your boss, but you prioritize uploading your Facebook status over it, you are procrastinating on the former task.

That said, if you delve deeper into procrastination, you will realize that it mainly involves postponing a more critical task to do something less important, but seemingly more attractive.

Continuing with the example of emailing your boss, you find using Facebook, more entertaining than sending a work-related email, so you automatically lean towards the former task more even though you are aware of the importance of sending that email.

Occasional procrastination is not too harmful. Let's face it, all of us have resorted to it at some point in our lives and procrastinate on specific tasks even regularly. As long as that isn't affecting our lives negatively or does not keep us from achieving our targets set for the day, that's okay.

Procrastination becomes problematic only when we engage in it for too long and resort to it every time we have something incredibly important to do.

Let us look at the different ways through which procrastination harms you.

How Procrastination Sabotages Your Life and Wellbeing

- Lowers Your Productivity: One of the first and most substantial effects of procrastination is that it hampers your productivity. Naturally, when you keep putting off your work until the last minute, you keep piling up work, and when you finally start to work on a task, you have so much on your plate that you end up tossing the plate out the window instead of working on anything at all. This keeps you from achieving your goals and moving closer to the many goals you have in life.

- Affects Your Discipline: When you keep delaying your tasks, you soon inculcate the habit of procrastination. On the surface, this may not seem too disturbing to you, but deep down, it disrupts your self-discipline. When you keep giving in to your temptations, you soon let go of the inner resistance that helps you combat your distractions. With time, your ability to maintain self-control weakens, and before you realize it, you completely lose the discipline you once had to do what is right and essential.

- Weakens Your Self-Confidence: With time, procrastination starts getting the better of you and makes you falter at everything you do because you have lost the ability to work hard and believe in yourself. This depletes your self-confidence, and you stop trying your hand at things you really want to do.
- Increases Your Stress Levels: Stress is often rooted in the inability to perform as you do or not fulfilling your goals. Naturally, when you keep falling behind schedule, have tons of tasks to do, feel unconfident, and cannot muster the courage to battle your temptations, your stress levels increase, which adds to your problems.
- Affects the Quality of Your Life: If you are governed by your temptations and not your own will, you keep succumbing to your meaningless desires. Instead of doing what is right and important, you keep working on pointless tasks and never achieve the sense of contentment and fulfillment, you need to feel good about yourself. Also, procrastination gets in the way of your routine chores, personal goals, and your responsibilities towards your loved ones. All of this affects the quality of your life and keeps you from living a truly amazing life.

Simply put, procrastination does not help you live a worthwhile life. It gets in the way of everything you plan and aspire to do, which only adds to your misery. To gain confidence, nurture discipline, become healthy and develop grit so you can gather better control of your life and live it on your terms, procrastination is one unhealthy habit you need to break. Let us move on to the next chapter and find out the first step you need to take to move closer to this goal.

BUILD THE INTENTION TO BREAK PROCRASTINATION

Every journey to a goal begins with a commitment, a commitment to improving, to have better control of your nerves, and to work with dedication and perseverance towards the end goal to eventually actualize it.

Without a firm commitment and a clear intention to achieve a certain goal, you are quite likely not going to move dedicatedly towards it. This is why your journey to breaking procrastination needs to begin with an unwavering commitment as well.

Accept Your Problem

To build a clear intention to resolve your problem, you first need to admit that you have a problem to address in the first place. Unless you acknowledge your problem, you will not fully realize its effects on your life and will not work faithfully to fix it. Accepting your problem becomes more comfortable when you focus on how it is affecting (read: sabotaging) your life. To do that, do the following:

- Analyze your daily routine starting from the time you wake up until you fall asleep and list down all the tasks you actually engage in. Do write down the time you devote to every job.

- Now assess the importance of every task on the list and think about what it helped you achieve that day. For instance, if you spent 3 hours researching on your final year philosophy project in college, what outcome did you realize after that research? Were you able to carry out meaningful research, or were you not so pleased with your findings primarily because you did not devote 3 full hours to researching on the topic? Think about whether or not every task you do daily helps you achieve anything meaningful in the end. If your end goal for the day is to earn $100, are you able to do it considering the time you spend on your work-related tasks?

- Also, think about how much time you actually spend on the tasks stated on the list and how much of that time is invested in other activities. If you spent 2 hours drafting a 200-word email to a potential investor in your business, think about what you actually did in those 2 hours. Were you actually thinking about the content of the email and research on it to ensure you draft a well-structured and effective email, or did you spend 1.5 hours using social media on your phone and spent only 30 minutes doing the actual task?

- Moreover, think about the tasks you plan to do daily, but somehow end up not doing. Write down those tasks and compare their importance and the outcomes they would have helped you achieved with the functions already put on the list. If you had intended to write a blog post for your blog, email some PR firms, pitch a proposal to a potential client, do some household chores including laundry and preparing dinner and had to spend 2 hours with your family, but you ended up only writing a blog post and doing laundry, why do you think that happened? What went wrong, and where did it go wrong that made you mess up your entire plan and not achieve your set targets for the day?

Once you have detailed out all the answers to the questions and have analyzed your routine, go through the account a few times, and within minutes, you will realize how prone you are to procrastination and how harmful it is for you. When you compare the results you achieve every day with the desired outcomes, you will automatically realize how your habit to postpone essential tasks and engage in something less meaningful but more attractive while you are working on an important task is actually a destructive habit that is only destroying your life. This realization will help you accept your problem.

It is crucial to make a verbal and then a handwritten declaration of this acceptance to put things out in the open. Say and write down, "I have a bad habit of procrastinating on important tasks, and I am going to work to break this habit steadfastly." Your declaration can be different, but the gist of it should be the same.

Make a Strong Commitment Backed by Compelling Whys

Now that you have acknowledged your problem and committed yourself to fix it, you need to solidify your commitment and strengthen it by pegging it to a compelling why. You need to have a convincing reason or even several reasons why you need to overcome your bad habit of procrastination, so you work with dedication towards your goal.

The whys associated with every goal motivate you to work towards its fulfillment because they are the reasons why you are chasing that goal. If there is no reason why you wish to break procrastination, why would you ever do that? If losing weight isn't relevant to you, why would you ever hit the gym and focus on healthy eating? To overcome procrastination, you need to figure out exactly why you wish to do it.

Close your eyes, or even keep them open if you want and think about the most significant issue you are facing in your life right now. It could be anything that makes you feel discontent, brings you any sort of pain. Is it keeping you from living a completely comfortable and happy life? It could be your struggle with losing weight or the obstacles you are experiencing in setting up your business or how you are battling depression and the urge to give in to it or anything else that is seriously adding friction to your life and restraining you from living how you genuinely wish to live.

Write down your findings, and if you recall your work routine and how much time you spend on actually meaningful tasks and those that only make you waste time, you will realize that procrastination is indeed a primary reason why you are struggling to achieve your desired goals. Think about how your life would change for the better if you mustered up the courage to fight your temptations and beat procrastination to do actual work for real. Write down those reasons and use them to fuel your motivation to work towards your commitment to overcome procrastination.

Set a Clear Goal

Now that you have a clearer understanding of why you need to overcome your urge to procrastinate and are more determined than before to work towards this very goal, set a clear intention to actually beat this bad habit. You can have several goals on your list that you would like to fulfill to live a more meaningful, happy life, but it is quite challenging to work on a handful of goals at once.

Remember, you only have a certain amount of willpower to work on a specific task, and that willpower depletes with every move you make towards a particular goal. Therefore, if you work for 3 hours straight on creating your company's website, you are likely to feel exhausted after that and will not be able to work on another high priority goal for another couple of hours.

To ensure you don't run short of willpower to work on anything meaningful at all, go slow and steady. Do make a list of the goals you would like to work on to become active, enthusiastic, and productive, but pick one important one from the list that you would like to work on first.

Ensure to make that goal as clear and specific as possible, so you know exactly what you are trying to achieve. If your goal is to improve your income, think about the amount of money you would like to earn every month and compare it with the amount you are actually making. If you procrastinate on keeping your house clean, think about how clean you want your home to be, and create a specific goal based on it. Once you have better clarity on your goal, write it down on your journal.

You now have a compelling reason to overcome procrastination. Next, you need to make an action plan to work enthusiastically towards this goal and battle every temptation that comes your way. The next chapter shows you exactly how to do that.

CREATE AN ACTION PLAN TO WORK TOWARDS YOUR GOAL

'A goal without a plan is just a wish.'- Antoine de Saint Exupery

A the goal is actually quite incomplete without a plan of action. You can never achieve your goal unless it is accompanied by a plan. Not having an action plan is often the reason why people fail to achieve their goals and end up starting from point zero every now and then. If you don't want that to happen to you again, this time devises a detailed action plan before working on your goal just like that.

Figure Out Why You Procrastinate

To create a foolproof action plan, you need to figure out the areas that need your utmost attention and effort. For that, you need to identify the significant reasons why you procrastinate to know what keeps you from working on your goal and waste time on pointless activities.

- Do you put off important tasks because you find them challenging?
- Do you delay doing your work because you lack an essential skill that can help you perform effectively and efficiently?
- Do you procrastinate because you feel easily attracted to more attractive and relaxing tasks such as watching movies or napping?
- Do you delay working on high priority tasks because you are scared of faltering and failing?
- Do you procrastinate because you overestimate the time you have to work on a task and feel too confident in your ability to do it successfully on time?
- Do you delay your tasks because you somehow underestimate the time it will take you to complete them?

The answers to these questions will give you more precise insight into the reasons why you procrastinate so much. Often, a combination of all these reasons leads to procrastination, and often, there is a specific reason attached to the delay of a particular task.

For instance, you may delay working on your statistics assignment because you find the subject tough; but, you may end up not submitting your business proposal to a prospective client on time because you thought it would only take you an hour to draft it and you kept putting it off until the last minute only to realize in the end that you need at least 5 hours to work on it.

Think about the reason why you have been procrastinating on the respective goal that you have just set. List down those reasons and go through them a few times to better understand how they compelled you to put off your substantial tasks for a long time. You need to create your plan of action in a manner that all the duties and steps make you manage these reasons. Then you don't give in to them again.

Set Deadline and Incremental Goals

Next, you need to set a deadline to start working on your goal and another deadline on which its fulfillment is due. A starting date is essential so that you don't keep putting off the target until the last minute and can battle the reason for overestimating the time to work on a task. The ending date is crucial because it helps you know when the goal is due, so you don't waste another minute and get down to business right away.

Think about how much time you would need to work on your respective goal and consider the pace at which you work. Once you have analyzed these factors, set a starting and ending date, and write it down.

You now know when you must start working on it and have to complete it in due course. Your next task is to set incremental goals so you can systematically work towards its fulfillment instead of taking it as ONE, BIG Goal!

Often, people get intimidated by a goal because it is too big and feels overwhelming, even one that is spread over a month. 30 days are a lot also, you know! To keep this intimidating feeling on the sidelines only, set incremental goals for yourself to slowly adjust yourself to this new transition, and steadily move towards the end destination. For instance, if your goal is to complete your 50,000-word e-book that you plan to self-publish on Amazon Kindle, but you keep procrastinating on it, then your daily/ weekly incremental goals could be:

- Write 1000 to 3000 words in week 1
- Write 4000 to 7000 words in week 2
- Write 8000 to 11000 words in week 3
- Write a total of 15000 words in the next 3 days
- Write another 5000 words in the next 3 days to make 20,000

This way, you would slowly move towards your ultimate goal of writing a 50,000-word e-book and get done with your goal in 3 to 4 months.

Create a Working Strategy during Your Peak Energy Time

Next, you need to create an effective strategy that helps you work on your incremental milestones and achieve them. First, determine your peak energy time. This is the time of the day you are brimming with energy and have the zeal to work on even the toughest of tasks.

Observe yourself and how you work on different tasks for a few days, and you will start to notice a somewhat similar pattern in the way you work on various tasks at different times of the day. This will give you a clearer understanding of your peak energy time.

Your goal now needs to be to work on your incremental milestones during this time window. If, however, your peak energy time is just an hour or two-hour-long, you need to increase it. In that case, you need to start working in small installments of 2 hours, each separated by an hour-long break instead of trying to do everything at once. To increase your peak energy time, take things slow and easy, and don't fret on completing all your tasks in one go. With time, your willpower will improve, and you will slowly inculcate the ability to work for long

You now have to draft a strategy on how to make the most of your peak energy time, so you get maximum output during that timeframe. Here is an effective plan that is quite likely to work in your favor:

- Think of the goal you plan to achieve during the first week. Having that in mind, identify the different things you have to work on to fulfill that milestone.

- Write down those tasks and then separate the high priority ones from the low priority tasks. The top priority tasks are all those that improve your productivity, and low priority ones are tasks that don't help you achieve your goals.

- Create a weekly to-do list that comprises of 4 to 5 high priority tasks that you have to do throughout the week to achieve your goal. Make sure the top priority tasks are assigned for your peak energy time.

- Break the weekly list into daily lists, and depending on your nature, pace, and the ability to handle different tasks, choose either of these two strategies. First, you do any one high priority and seemingly harsh task right when the day starts. This is also known as 'eat an ugly frog' strategy and is an excellent technique to kick start your day and boost your productivity. However, if that is too overwhelming for you, start with a seemingly more effortless task and gradually move towards a toughie at the end of the day or even the end of the week, so you have trained yourself to work consistently by then.

- Separate all your tasks with breaks in between so you get some time to rest and rejuvenate after working on an assignment for even an hour. Some people, especially those who have trouble concentrating on a task for even 30 minutes straight, work for 15 minutes then take a quick 5-minute break. You can even choose this strategy if it suits you. It is also known as the 'Pomodoro Technique' named after Italian chef Cirillo Pomodoro's tomato-shaped timer. Pomodoro is Italian for tomato. As the chef used his tomato-shaped timer to improve his time management skills and worked on 3 to 4 installments of 20 minutes each, the 'Pomodoro Technique' was created based on this. You also can work in this manner to make things easier for yourself.
- Identify all the probable distractions that lure you away from your essential chores and look for ways to manage them. For instance, if your hand unintentionally moves towards the TV remote every time you sit to work on your book, that there is your distraction that you need to overcome. If you are tempted to hit your snooze button and sleep for another hour every time you have to read articles for your thesis, that is your temptation that you have to work on. List down your distractions and look for effective ways to manage them. If you are tempted to sleep, maybe force yourself to get up and walk for 100 steps to charge up yourself, so you work on the high priority task. If the TV distracts you, take it off the wall and hide it in the attic so you have nothing distracting in your room and can focus better on working. Often, our distractions are associated with the environment we sit to work in. Bringing some changes in the surrounding is often the trick to manage distractions and increase our productivity.
- Next, you need to start working on the first task on your list and just do it without overthinking it. It is best to plan it beforehand right when you are creating your weekly/ daily to-do list, so you know how to execute it at that time. When it is time for you to work on your to-do list, pick the first task, and complete it right away. You don't have any time to think about it because that would trigger procrastination once again. Avoid that by just doing that task to save yourself from any trouble later on. If it helps, encourage yourself to work on it for 5 to 10 minutes only and keep going like that for a while. Referred to as the '5 Minute Hack', this trick mostly works well in helping you engage in a seemingly tough task and completing at least one part of it successfully.

Work on these guidelines consistently for a few days, and in a couple of weeks, you will get the hang of the routine and nurture a habit of it. You now have to keep working on your weekly to-do lists to achieve your incremental milestones, one after another, to move closer towards your destination.

Learn to Settle for Good Enough

Often, people who have the habit of chasing perfectionism and trying to do everything correctly, find it incredibly hard to achieve their set targets. If you are a perfectionist or use perfectionism as an excuse not to work on your plan of action, you are quite likely to fall in the same trap when you try to overcome your urge to procrastinate.

Now that you have learned how to commit yourself to this goal and know how to craft an effective action plan, you need to train yourself not to allow perfectionism to take over you.

To become a doer and achieve your targets, learn to settle for good enough results, and not exhaust yourself trying to achieve 100% results because nothing is really perfect. Perfectionism is a myth because nothing can ever be perfect. There will always be some room left for improvement, something that could have been better; some aspect that you could have paid more attention to and some area which, if you could have worked harder on, would have helped you achieve better results. The truth is this is because of a glitch in your mind. You need to fix that glitch to block your negative thoughts pertinent to overthinking and perfectionism.

Here is how you can learn to settle for good enough, overcome your tendency to chase perfectionism and slowly overcome procrastination for good:

- Whenever you start doing a task, think of the set target before tending to that chore.
- Go through the steps of the tasks and set a specific time limit to work on every level. If you have to create a business logo for a client and the steps involved include researching for inspiration for an hour, working on the logo for 2 hours, and making sure it complements the client's ideology and demands then make sure to work on every step for the designated timeframe only.
- Start working on the steps and make sure to spend only the designated time on every level, not even a minute more. If somehow you are unable to achieve a specific stage in the set time, move to the next step. If you cannot move forward without completing the previous step, take a break and tend to that chore after a few hours or at the same time the next day.
- Once you are done with a task, analyze your performance, and tell yourself how happy you are with the outcome even if you were able to achieve 50% to 60% of the set target. Smile and keep telling yourself repeatedly how pleased you are with yourself. If you do it intentionally a few times, you will eventually be happy

with your performance. That said, do identify your weaknesses and work on them to achieve even better results the next time.

If you consistently work on these steps and train yourself to achieve your set targets within the set timeframe and not spend extra time on a task, you will eventually learn to settle for good enough. Your next task is to further strengthen your focus, so you work with sheer dedication towards your objective.

REINFORCE YOUR FOCUS TO COMPLETE GOALS ON TIME

Your focus determines how far along you will move towards the pursuit of your goal like an anonymous quote states,

'When you focus on what you want, everything else falls away.'

If your focus is right and you are attentive towards precisely what you want, everything else on the sidelines stops distracting you. When you know you have to earn $5000 by the end of the month, you will not care whether you have to work for 6 hours a day or whether you have to work out in the cold. You know what you have to achieve, and you see nothing but your goal. This is the killer focus you need to actualize your goal, stay disciplined with temptations all around, and beat procrastination.

While the strategies taught in the previous chapters help you become focused, here are some more techniques designed primarily to sustain and increase your focus on your goal.

Visualize Achieving Your Goal

Visualization is an incredibly valuable activity that makes you consciously focus on your goal by training your subconscious to concentrate on the end goal. It requires you to imagine yourself achieving your goal. When you visualize yourself as a winner in your mind's eye, you train your mind to think positively. This creates many positive thoughts in that direction that draw positive experiences towards you, helping you achieve your goal.

Every morning when you wake up and each night before going to bed, think of your end goal and imagine that you have achieved it. Add as many details as you would like to add in this creative visualization and enjoy imagining that scenario for 10 to 15 minutes.

Also, slowly inculcate the habit to visualize yourself working on every task 10 minutes before doing it. So if you have to attend a seminar and present a speech on it, imagine you are at the venue and are delivering an impactful statement. This helps you map out the task in your head before actually doing it and trains your mind to work on it effectively, which increases your chances of success.

Visualization practiced daily helps you become an optimistic thinker and makes you hopeful of a bright tomorrow, which only improves your chances of success.

Become Process Oriented

As important as it is to be goal-oriented, it is equally important to focus on the process, the journey that takes you to the end goal. When pursuing a goal, we are likely to stumble and make a few mistakes. In that case, many of us often end up criticizing ourselves and quitting that goal altogether. This mostly happens because you fail to enjoy the journey that takes you forward towards your goal.

An excellent technique to ensure you aren't too harsh on yourself in difficult times is to become process-oriented. For that, you need to take an interest in every step of the process. Celebrate even your littlest of accomplishments to feel proud of yourself. Make sure to write down how you perform on every little to significant milestone and treat yourself to something nice every time you accomplish a set target even if it is something small as sending emails to potential clients. If you were able to do a task from your to-do list attentively and battle the distractions that try to entice you, you did a great job and deserve a nice treat to celebrate that. Also, every time you have a tough task on your list, set a reward beforehand. Indulge in that treat once you have accomplished that task to enjoy your accomplishment and the process that takes you to your goals.

Besides, track your performance to become better aware of your weaknesses and setbacks, so you improve on your shortcomings. Also, try different ways of doing the same task to find out the one technique that yields the best results. When you take a better interest in the process, you enjoy it more and happily work on even the difficult tasks to achieve your goal.

Steer Clear of Naysayers

One of the biggest distractions almost all of us experience is the naysayers around us. If there is even a single robust and negative influence in your life that keeps telling you how you cannot achieve your goal, that may be the reason why you fail to accomplish your goals.

When people keep telling you how your goal is way too difficult for you to accomplish; or how it is better to relax now and work later; or how you have been failing at achieving your earlier goals, so there is no point in setting more goals now, you are quite likely to fall in that trap. The moment you believe what the negative influences around you tell you, you trigger your habit of procrastination, and before you realize you are happily wasting away time doing pointless tasks.

If you want to stick to the routine you have created for yourself to slowly rid yourself of procrastination, you need to get rid of these naysayers from your environment to become more focused on your goal. Determine all these negative influences and how they impact you, and slowly distance yourself from them. Make a list of all the different people in your social circle, particularly those you spend the most time with. Think about the influence they have on you. Do you experience some sort of bitterness, negativity, frustration, and stress during or after you hang out with those people? Do you find yourself feeling demotivated and leaning towards your temptations and addictions after you have spent some time with some people? If yes, those people are the naysayers you need to reduce how much time you spend with them.

Being around naysayers only debilitates your self-confidence and sets off your tendency to lean towards distractions to manage your stress, boredom, and any other issue that you are going through in life. You really don't want that sort of negativity going around in your life because that only takes you away from what you aspire to achieve.

Now that you are well aware of how certain people impact you, slowly build the courage to distance yourself from them. Yes, you will have to be firmer with yourself and even with those people for some time, but with time and consistency, you will learn to manage the time spent with them and the way they influence you. You will have to stop taking the calls of certain people, block them on your social media, excuse yourself from particular social gatherings and make similar other changes to your routine and the way you interact with people to ensure you can block off their negative effect on your life. With some people, you will even have to be firm, but that is okay; you will see the fruits of doing this soon enough.

While you do that, surround yourself with positive people to feel inspired at all times. Just as negative influences distract you from your goal, positive impacts encourage you to work on your aspirations and nurture your motivation, enthusiasm, and a positive mindset. You need such influences in your life to arduously work towards the fulfillment of your goals and ardently work on your action plan to eventually overcome procrastination for good.

Also, look for any such person in your social circle who is working on a goal similar to yours, both the intent to overcome procrastination and the other purpose you have set to fuel your motivation to become disciplined. Ask that person to work alongside you so the two of you can serve as each other's accountability partners. An accountability friend is someone who keeps an eye on you, and your performance towards your goals keeps your triggers in check and motivates you to continually stick to your plan. This helps you manage your temptations successfully and do what is right. For instance, if you have a colleague who has been meaning to start his own marketing agency, but has been procrastinating on that task in one way or another, talk to him about your goal and work towards your respective goals together. This way, both of you can keep the other on his/ her toes and help each other in fulfilling your objectives.

Apart from doing the above, read positive books focused on self-development and listen to inspirational talks, podcasts and lectures on these topics to provide your mind with healthy mental food and encourage it to become more attentive towards your goal. You need to continually make sure that you think positively because if you direct your focus towards the right things, you gather inner courage to block all sorts of external negativity. When you are strong and optimistic for a better future from within, outside influences don't disturb you that much, and you can easily combat them. So ensure to read something positive every day, so you focus on your end goal.

Do Things You Enjoy

Also, to do all of the above, pay attention to your needs, and do things you actually enjoy. Often, procrastination is your way to vent out the in-built frustration because you haven't been able to do something you enjoy. If you have just been working hard for a long time and haven't done anything enjoyable for long, you are likely to lean towards meaningless activities. This can then trigger your habit of procrastinating and create more significant problems for you.

An excellent way to keep that from happening is to devote some time to your needs of enjoyment and entertainment occasionally. Make it a daily or weekly ritual to engage in some enjoyable activity such as painting, dancing, listening to music, or anything else that mitigates your stress and helps you breathe. When you consistently spend some quality me-time, you feel better and content with yourself and can quickly motivate yourself to work on your high priority tasks on time.

Remember, it takes time, courage, and perseverance to achieve your goal, so keep taking baby steps to climb up the ladder.

CONCLUSION

Thank you again for reading this book! I hope this book was able to help you to learn how to stop procrastinating through the examples and practices explained in this book.

You can find my other work on Amazon and other stores, as a paperback, but also as E-Books:

1) Mindfulness Meditation: A Beginner's Guide to Yoga Meditation

2) Mindfulness: Yoga And Meditation, Simple Beginners Guide To Stress Relief And Happiness

3) Mindfulness: The Benefits of Meditation, a Beginner's Guide to Peace of Mind in Your Everyday Life

4) Procrastination Cure: How to Use Mindfulness Meditation to Stop Procrastinating

If you like this book, please follow me on:
Facebook https://www.facebook.com/gmposi/
Twitter https://twitter.com/george_posi
Instagram https://www.instagram.com/georgemposi
YouTube https://www.youtube.com/channel/UCmffykN4Iq8TY_1yyUWdoeA

Share how did you like my work on Facebook or Twitter with your friends!
Visit my blog site https://georgemposi.com

Finally, if you enjoyed this book, would you be kind enough to leave an honest review for it on Amazon.

ABOUT THE AUTHOR

George M. Posi is an internet author and publisher and experienced entrepreneur. For the past 30 years, he has been the owner and manager of his own IT company. Five years ago, he started his journey towards mindfulness and began to seek new challenges. Then he promised himself that all business that he does must be done with respect and kindness to himself and to others.

George M. Posi started writing and publishing books as a way to reach as many people he can, to help others commit to this value in every area of their lives through self-development, including health, fitness, emotions, mindset, and spirituality.

He is grateful for all the experiences that he had in his life this first 55 years. All of those, positive and negative, helped him learn valuable life lessons. His life has since truly changed. His mission is to give back and serve others and to be a positive example of the unlimited possibilities that life offers for those that are genuinely committed to seeking mindfulness in their everyday activities.

Visit the website https://georgemposi.com, as well as YouTube channel Mindfulness Journey, where he openly and passionately shares all his experiences that have made a measurable difference to the quality of his life and will for yours as well.

Topics that George M. Posi writes about are Health and Fitness, Yoga, Mind and Beliefs, Emotions, Mission and Purpose, Productivity, Spirituality, and more...